WORDS, WORLD

POEMS

DANIEL CORRIE

BLUE HORSE PRESS   REDONDO BEACH, CALIFORNIA   2016

WORDS, WORLD

DANIEL CORRIE

Blue Horse Press
P.O. Box 7000 - 760
Redondo Beach,
California 90277

Copyright © 2016 by Daniel Corrie.
All rights reserved.
Printed in the United States of America.

Cover art: *Prairie Cycle (Falcon)*
by Suzanne Stryk

Editors: Jeffrey and Tobi Alfier
Blue Horse Press logo: Amy Lynn Hayes

ISBN 978-0692699263

ACKNOWLEDGEMENTS

Poems from this book appeared in the following magazines, several having been revised since their appearance:

Hudson Review: "Of Being and Becoming" and "The Struggle to Exist"
Kenyon Review: "Rising, Opening, Encompassing"
Measure: "World"
Shenandoah: "The Day and the Night"
Southwest Review: "Words"
Virginia Quarterly Review: "The Dancing Bear"

"Words" received the first-place 2011 Morton Marr Poetry Prize, selected by Jennifer Clarvoe.

Poems from this book were reprinted in the anthologies *The Gulf Stream: Poems of the Gulf Coast* (edited by Brent House and Jeff Newberry) and *The Southern Poetry Anthology: Georgia* (edited by Paul Ruffin and William Wright).

For William Wright

Table of Contents

Rising, Opening, Encompassing	1
The Day and the Night	3
The Dancing Bear	4
Words	12
World	13
Of Being and Becoming	14
The Struggle to Exist	19

Rising, Opening, Encompassing

> *The universe is the only text*
> *without a context.*
> *— Thomas Berry*

Through different trees, wind becomes different sounds.
The pines become the wind's sound, here. I hear it.

Again the creek leads me along its seam, from my name.
Its artery opens out from trees, to a heart of water.

No identity will be time-honored. It will be time.
I feel mine. It is blood-honored. It is change-honored.

It is solitude's language. It is oblivious sunlight
falling over leaves. Their ancient need greened to feel it.

Monumental time pairs into wings, flexing frail bones.
Wings open like meaning under meaningless sky.

Again geese lift from the pond I once knew well.
Their wings beat. Their harsh calls tear at the air

of my rising. We rise on our wingthrusts belonging
in our migration. In summoning's wingwind, syllables

whisper through the rush of more slurring syllables.
The lines of being recite themselves. The primal poem

scores the lines of flyways through impulses born
knowing their courses, as creeks follow courses.

The one wing eclipsed the sky, wing of millions
of wings, shadow's thunder of pigeons flown

gone into change-honor, accepted by change-honor.
The disembodying wind calls my embodied mind.

Time is the cadence falling. It falls calmly as light
over leaves' incarnation, carnage, reincarnation.

The pond is left as ripples stilling, evaporating
from my knowing. My heartbeats count the tides

of blood's migrations, pulses echoing out into older
iambics of nights beating into days, in the wordless odes.

The Day and the Night

> *Familiar, transient* . . . .
> —*Marcus Aurelius*

I dream the quiet moccasin cuts its path
on a shimmering surface. New apples gleam
in the orchard I remember. The horizon's seam
glimmers, a thread's line stitched through cloth,

its pattern bleaching out in sunlight. The smell
of mown grass falls like sleep. The sun centers,
providing sky the meaning of noon. A canna enters
into summer, becoming the color of its spell.

Then I dream the evening purples. Fading follows
across the clouds. Minutes darken, graying past
acres of a field where a tireless tractor plows
the unremembering earth. Horizon's Venus glows.

The dreamless parsecs float. Night abides unlost,
unknowing of its stars, of days, of poetry, of cost.

The Dancing Bear

> *You have shown me an image*
> *of strange prisoners.*
> −Plato

i.

In some fashion, they taught the bear to dance,
to guzzle Cokes and beers, to swallow cigarettes.
Kept in a cage beside the Texaco, it brought in customers.
Or lost in that cage beneath the stars,
it sprawled in drunken sleep with restless dreams,
clawing at nothing or clawing
at all Mississippi.

ii.

Last night's storm broke down
the old elm. Again, chaos paused to give a clue.
Little's to be done,
except for roots to change
into the earth they'd known.
I'll guide its former height,
shepherding it to firewood and smoke.

Like footfall after footfall,
days and nights fall
following through the feeling

of being born
into a prefigurement
of a world that time whispers
can't be.

Season can follow season
as hammerfall after hammerfall,
forging time.

Too soon to learn our lessons, even
for a life instilled with grace enough
to bless a cell it can't venture from
or to comprehend the random visitor who tarries
to feed a burning cigarette
through a cage's padlocked gate.

iii.

Again for me, page by page,

Plato imagines
the really real. The words
might become worlds, again,
for a while.

For me, drowsy with reading,
my shoulder blades propped
against the bed's headboard,

his womb-cave of words
shifts with his prisoners

sprawled in their chains,
backs propped against rock,
eyes following shadows crossing
his dream-cave's gritty wall.

Word-ink rises from depths
of a page's paper shallows.
Beyond ink-shadows,

the page is white as the blinding
scrim of perfection's glare.

Other days I've read
ink's black letters blotting

into red, again bleeding
the upraised voice

of a doer of miracles, young sojourner

from perfection's placeless place
of timeless time,

man-god preaching on a hill

until a later page's ink of scripture
will raise him beyond
worldly wounds.

Sometimes you'll ask words to tell you
why this suffering?

Sometimes you'll hear wordlessness repeating

cancer's X-ray shadow –
Alzheimer's ceaseless dream –
the sleeper's veering car –

spilled milk, spilled blood –

spilled randomness –

Sometimes wordlessness is repeating

giving suffering
to each other –

as inheritance, as legacy –

as blind doing – as choice –

The wordlessness will be repeating
how does the twisted body
untwist its seeing?

how does the twisted life
untwist its living?

iv.

My child's vocabulary
couldn't catch the words
to think *unholy* –
how unholy you look out at me

until I recollect a childish way of gazing
upon some brute unholiness

as commonplace,
roadside freakshow
beyond a ditch where cars speed past,

great darkness growling groggily
beyond the cyclone fence –
safely, safely locked away, it seemed –

where my young parents,
grown tired from traveling,
stretch their legs and hold my hand,

suddenly swept far
beyond the high and dark blue dome
of memory.

I see us,
three shadows in twilight,
near our bad dreams' fence-line
laughing and pointing.

v.

In sleep's currents, I feel
ink and starlessness ripple
through the black

of my pupils widening.
Blackness pours, shivering, its thick
fur flowing.

In umbra's deepening,
I hear the bear

emerging – rumbling
I am

you – I am
one
of all

the scouring selves
beyond your cage
of self –

come into me

into the river – river hunting
tirelessly over rocks

*as I hunt
through its wash —*

*salmon's need hunting
for the feeling of someplace
spawning through
scales, fins, gills —*

through push, thrust, leap — to push

*as the salmon — to thrust —
to leap
as the salmon*

*through river's roar —
river arching,
its back bristling*

in cascading,

*twisting in sun into
translucence, through*

the hunting world —

The hour is cool in mud's bed,
when the victory of spray
creams through water
over the viscous eggs of the salmon.

Eggs drink in, dreaming in
their own outset under the shadows
of the siring shapes tiring

as bright scales dull, suddenly sickly,
peeling away, their suddenness
peeling away.

vi.

Sometimes like horizon's distant, muffled thunder,
the bear's wordlessness whispers

can you answer?

can you make more out of time
than time's cage?

vii.

Sometimes the bear's wordlessness whispers

leave yourself

leave your cage

come into me where
there is no answer

Words

> *"Meaning" is a constructed*
> *human dimension.*
> — Meredith Sabini

I almost heard. It built through me, alone.
Words rose like stones. Words stilled, building the poem.
It was a temple for an afternoon.

I left the swingset rusting on the lawn
that was my childhood calling through the poem.
Each word was pure and far. Each was alone

as morning fell on faces, then was gone
into the mourning that became the poem.
It was a temple for an afternoon

of perfect columns that remained unseen.
Mind's columns built a time that was the poem.
It hadn't shown its words were words alone,

as weeks dissolved through years, like misting rain.
A human meaning rose to be the poem
and stood, a temple for an afternoon.

It lasted with me. It was gone too soon.
Words blurred through pages, paging past each poem
through time beyond a poem's time alone,

beyond all temples of words' afternoon.

World

> *It is only a little planet*
> *But how beautiful it is.*
> *— Robinson Jeffers*

Earth birthed the root, the flight, the flow, the bone.
Behemoth granite breached through cloud, to be the prayer
that was the being of its afternoon.

The osprey dove through oceanic dawn
to fish tide's tireless pitch and roar of prayer.
Earth birthed the root, the flight, the flow, the bone

swarming to thunderheads of pigeons, flown
into the quiet of wind's whispered prayer.
Into the being of an afternoon,

wind rippled miles of marsh grass, shivered grain,
shaped snow, dunes, fire, and cloud, as words shape prayer.
Earth birthed the root, the flight, the flow, the bone

as earth blushed red with iron, as veins ran
pulsing with iron through the blood of prayer
feeling the being of the afternoon.

Sequoias soared to heights of looming green
to stand in grandeur of their wordless prayer,
earth birthing root and flight and flow and bone

to be the prayer, to be the afternoon.

Of Being and Becoming

> *I am divided up in time, whose*
> *order I do not know.*
> —*Augustine*

Its insect mouth half formed, never to feed,
one mayfly will be born in spring
from the cool creek

to find the feel
of its veined transparency of wings
beating to climb,

needing what was never taught,
joining the sexual cloud
of its swarming kind.

Each will roughly clasp or be clasped,

their flurry hurrying
to clasp their winged lifetime's
single day.

Sometimes from fathoms of sleep,
I rise swimming
from my forgetting

ancestral fins, scales, gills,
feeling water turn to wind, pulling me
from the swarming plankton's
wide, bluegreen womb of water.

Now water narrows, birth canal
through forest into clearing.

From the field's gleaming
seam of creek, I walk
in my scuffed boots and mud-spattered jeans,

feeling sweat soak the back
of my neck's binocular strap.
Sweat gives me salt's taste

of something almost as lost

as dimmest memory of tasting
breath in sun-dimming depths.

Fifty years have been
too sudden for knowing

where I've emerged walking,
looking, listening – then to hear

the scream, again and again,
to look up to the high hawk's
broad wings cocked,

riding the rise of morning's
warming air, higher with each circle.

It screams its hunter's ownership
of the territory beneath
its called claims.

This March's hunter
will die to a future's twin hunter
climbing other mornings' circles,

screaming the same scream.

In one of the dreams,

a god stood, totem unchanging,
shape risen to a pillar,
perfection's looming monolith

beyond years' rains melting
temples' ruined, toppled columns.

I've seen a column rise into sky,

column of a forest's smoke.
Each tree was fire's pillar.

Smoke's columns soon drift, form hazing
as if forgetting itself,

as a dark sky will clear

to stars, like leaves' cooling embers
drifting through a night's air.

A creek's course will dry to earth-scar,
left like a memory of water running.

Each of my creeds fell like sunlight
in a creek's water braiding

sometime through time's
long season of making,
unmaking, making.

Again blind rain will need
the arid creek bed to flood

re-carving its shape,
ancient shape
of skin-changing snake –

shape writhing in its shedding.

Time: transfiguring

triptych of past, present, and future –
Great swarm of triunes

of beginnings, middles, and endings –
I stand in the memory of water rushing
one morning through sunlight,

lost creek unlost
where I crossed, stopping ankle deep,

kept in its going – keeping its going,

where I was – where I am.

Great form
of transformation –

Enduring shape
of metamorphosis –

Sometimes I hear the parable
of my past reciting me
like a future.

Sun-filled in my seeing,
creek's current was a clarity

like the good. Its vein of feeling
might course as clearly

through a life's blood-blush –

through blood's reddening horizons

of duskdawn into duskdawn
of now into now.

The Struggle to Exist

i. Seedfall

There is a solitary oak
in Georgia
in a soy field.

In spring, its leaves open,

wide breadth of old limbs greening,
shading the few
family gravestones,

each stone blackened as though
charred by years.

Two stones have lifted, tilting
above the longevity
of roots probing.

Past field and tree line,
forests of each tree
among trees

will fight each summer's
silent fight,

tree competing with tree,

each trunk pressing
up, limbs
pressing out,

branch tips probing
for sunlit gaps, for each oasis
of a sunbeam falling
through green shafts,

each leaf needing
to feel the sun
light up its green
like a Chinese lantern's
paper screen –

to win sunlight –

to steal sunlight –

to own the sun –

The old oak stands apart
on its island of graves

to be with the sun –

being with the sun –

where it once fell, acorn
in the random rain
of all acorns.

ii. Timefall

Time's four-syllabled
mantra recircles:

dawn noon dusk night –

Time's four-worded
mantra recircles:

spring summer autumn winter –

Emerging from winter's
thawed, sodden soil,

a line of oaks, naked of leaves,
stands against sky
beyond consciousness,

their years holding them
concentric in their cores,

growth rings keeping
their pasts living
without mind's reliving,

rooted beyond boys
who called and ran

somewhere near,
then were gone.

Two million years

doubled a brain
into one mind's three pounds

cradled in my skull –

brain of a species
suddenly glimpsing

existence's shape
like shrapnel

in its starry explosion –

species suddenly glimpsing
a world circling

through the verdant eras'
sunlight showering

into the fall
of eclipsing eras'

annuluses of annulment.

Life posed itself
the riddle of two halves

torn apart into searching
for each other.

Then the seven billion
surge, cresting – river
of hungers.

The brain that blindly
evolves itself
asks itself

each successive riddle

past each answer
of each epoch risen
as the next

pylon uplifting, arch extending

from the oldest river's
tangled bank

to somewhere
cloudily imagined.

It is mind's lunge –

untried flyway's outset.

All possible forkings
will converge, veering

into the single, narrow
arc of acts.

The bridge extends
building itself, pointing toward
the one future –

before flyways' scoring
of the sky

will fade, pathways misting
from the elder instincts
of wings that had teemed –

before the tangled banks
of rivers will untangle,
withering –

before male and female
will uncouple, falling
into vanishing –

before a moment will dissolve
among dark parsecs'
unfelt, unmarked durations

of flocks of rocks

floating through solar winds'
flyways of dead drift.

In flyways of orbits,
satellites gleam in sun,

lenses aimed down
on the blue and green world's

cyclones' swirls
like fingerprints.

iii. Embodiment

Spasm of the life
of a fly taking flight
on birth-damp wings

or of thought rising through
some version of meaning –

One life blinks into living

into its version
of the inevitable world

to glimpse landscapes
suddenly familiar, apart

from the long preludes.

The merlin rises
on predatory wings
like an act of thanks,

to ride sky's thermals
tethered, recircling

in the rule
of the ring
of impulse and instinct.

An animal rose wingless
into skies in its skull

circling wider, hunting

through dreams
too wide for its world.

Pine of my South –

given a name
for its dozen-inch needles,

longleaf was all but taken.

Again on our farm,
I walked under the few
acres of survivors
grown old and fat.

I passed each scar,
each trunk's wound

still deep from the rushed
harvests for turpentine's
once-brisk market.

Each gash rose
to the height
of a man's upstretched reach,

until I walked past the one
that slowed me, showed me
its empty niche waiting

as though summoning
to shelter a relic
grown holy.

Pine shape before me
stood for me,

risen analogical –

meaning-bearer –

scar shrine
opening its scar arch,

recess where I placed
one of its own
new-fallen cones.

I remember a day under
other trees when I stopped
to drink water.
Out through tall grass,

I could make out
a remnant path
other feet had left
nearly unseeable,

where breeze tousled leaves
scattering light, dappling ground
with bright ghosts

of coins, unhoardable.

Born into the setting
of a life's
time and place –
into place risen

into sometime's setting
like the sun,

we might become

a form of thanks.

Time gives touch.

Time is the giver

of a companion
who becomes
the shape of life

and the rest of seasons.

My wife and I will look up

and again trade words

about an evening's
light folding
into violet clouds' veer,

as our reach of nights
will stretch into promises

of the reach of returning,
quiet light.

Birth canal of becoming

will guide sun and moon to follow
their course above trees.

Flocks will pass over trees

flying into their living,

filling their flyways
of becoming.

The great losses
must be the great guides
to finding.

I've read words
of someone called a saint – *It is
love alone that gives
worth to all things* –

Birth canal
into future – Course

of generations of being
will follow human being –

greed into greed –
need into need –

attempting into attempting –

love into love –

a spanning bridge
of recognition

in coming to love
the teeming otherness
of the world we are –

into the anciently fresh
worth of the world

in its birthing forth.

About the Author

Daniel Corrie's first full-length book of poems is near completion. His poems have appeared in *The American Scholar, Birmingham Poetry Review, Greensboro Review, Hudson Review, Image, Kenyon Review, Measure, Missouri Review, The Nation, New Criterion, Shenandoah, Southern Review, Southwest Review, Terrain.org, Virginia Quarterly Review,* with poems selected for four anthologies and for *Verse Daily*. Aralia Press published a chapbook of his poetry. One of his poems received the first-place 2011 Morton Marr Poetry Prize. He and his wife live on their farm in rural Georgia.

www.ingramcontent.com/pod-product-compliance
Lightning Source LLC
Chambersburg PA
CBHW032106040426
42449CB00007B/1202